Chips

Anne Mountfield

Blackwell Education

Text copyright © Anne Mountfield 1989
Illustrations copyright © Basil Blackwell Ltd 1989

First published 1989
Basil Blackwell Ltd
108 Cowley Road
Oxford OX4 1JF
UK

British Library Cataloguing in Publication Data
Mountfield, Anne
  How food begins.
  1. Food – For children
  I. Title   II. Series
  641.3

  ISBN 0–631–90338–0
  ISBN 0–631–16633–5: v.2: cased
  ISBN 0–631–90334–8: v.2: pbk

Illustrated by Corinne Burrows
Typeset in 20 on 30 pt Century by
Columns of Reading
Printed in Great Britain by MacLehose & Partners, Portsmouth

2

Contents

What do you like best?
Sausages and chips?
Fish and chips?
Or burger and chips?

Guess what?

Chips begin . . .

. . . as little potatoes under the ground.

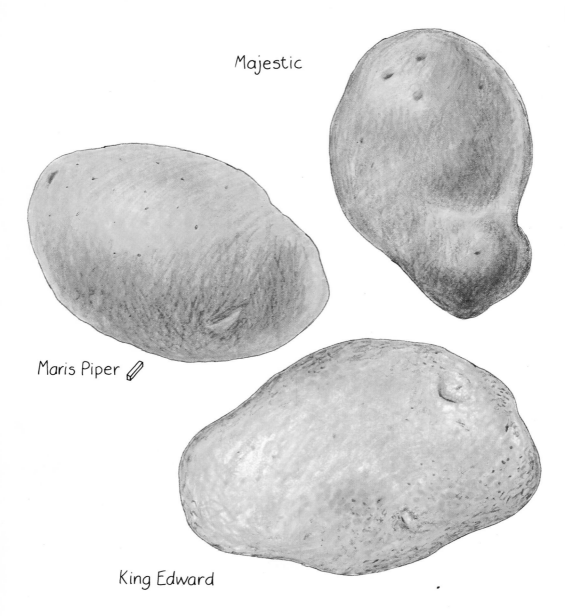

Majestic

Maris Piper

King Edward

Here are some different kinds of potato.
Do they look the same?
Which kinds make the best chips?

Red Craig Royal

Desiree

Home guard

Pentland Crown

Golden Wonder

Seed potatoes are called tubers.
They make roots in the ground.

In spring the plants grow leaves and
    flowers.
The leaves make food for the
    new potatoes that grow under the
    ground.

The first new potatoes are very small.

If they grow in the ground until
August, they will be the
right size for chips.

It is easy to dig the potatoes out.
But it can be hard work to pick them up.
The potatoes go to the chip factory in a
    truck.

The potatoes are still very
dirty so they are washed.
Any green potatoes are thrown away.
Green potatoes are bad for you.

This factory sells some potatoes to
  shops.
The potatoes come in different sizes.
How does this machine sort them out?

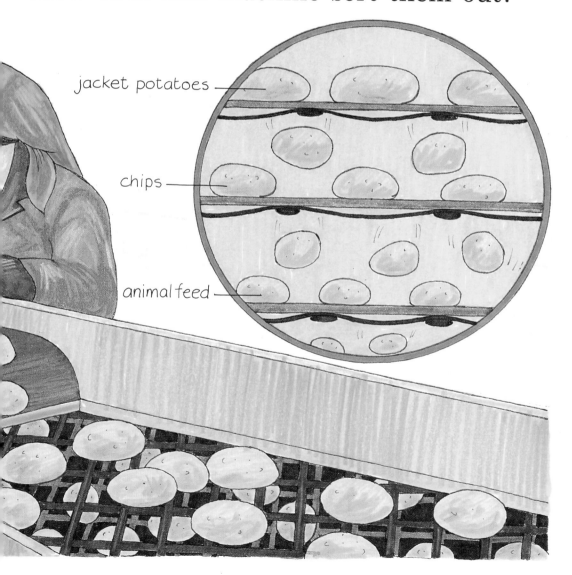

jacket potatoes

chips

animal feed

How do we peel potatoes at home?
This machine peels potatoes for chips.
It peels them with steam.

The wet potatoes roll down into the
    cutter.
It cuts them into chip shapes.

Then the chips roll into hot water.
They do not stay there very long.
When they come out the chips are
hot and wet.

The next machine shakes them dry.
Clouds of steam rise from the machine.

Then the chips go into the
    frying machine.
The fat in the machine is very hot.

The chip factory smells like a big
chip shop.
It makes you feel very hungry.

These chips are going to be frozen.
They are going into a tunnel.

A very cold wind blows along the tunnel.
It freezes the chips until they are hard.

The frozen chips go to the shops in bags.
You have to finish cooking them before
you eat them.

How many ways have you eaten
potatoes?

Why should you not eat too many chips?

You could try growing potatoes yourself.
Here is a way to do it:

clear container

charcoal

gravel

compost

black paper

Index